Go the F**k Back to Work!

Rhymes to Inspire Our
Contemptible Congress to
Just Do Its F**king Job

by L.K. Peterson
illustrated by Tom Hachtman

Front cover by Tom Hachtman
Artwork first appeared @ inxart.com
Coloring by Martin Kozlowski

For more on Now What Media Books,
please visit nowwhatmedia.com/nowwhatbooks.html

What this country needs is more working men and fewer politicians.

— *Will Rogers*

Talk is cheap — except when Congress does it.
— *Cullen Hightower*

Term limits aren't enough. We need jail.

— *P.J. O'Rourke*

With as many days off as a Frenchman

And many more times the perks,

On those rare days you are in session,

Please go the f**k back to work.

Governance sure gets frustrating

When neck-deep in red tape you bob.

Then again, nobody forced you to take it,

So just do the f**king job!

Shedding crocodile tears about gridlock

While choking back theatrical sobs,

Isn't accomplishing anything useful, so

Just do your f**king jobs

The chattering class may revere you

Or revel in revealing your quirks.

But giving interviews isn't your job here

So get the f**k back to work!

Swept into national office

By a bloodthirsty home-district mob,

You're supposed to now do something,

Like, maybe your f**king job?

You likely campaigned on a promise

To cut through the Washington murk.

We'd like to see somebody do that, so

Get the f**k to work

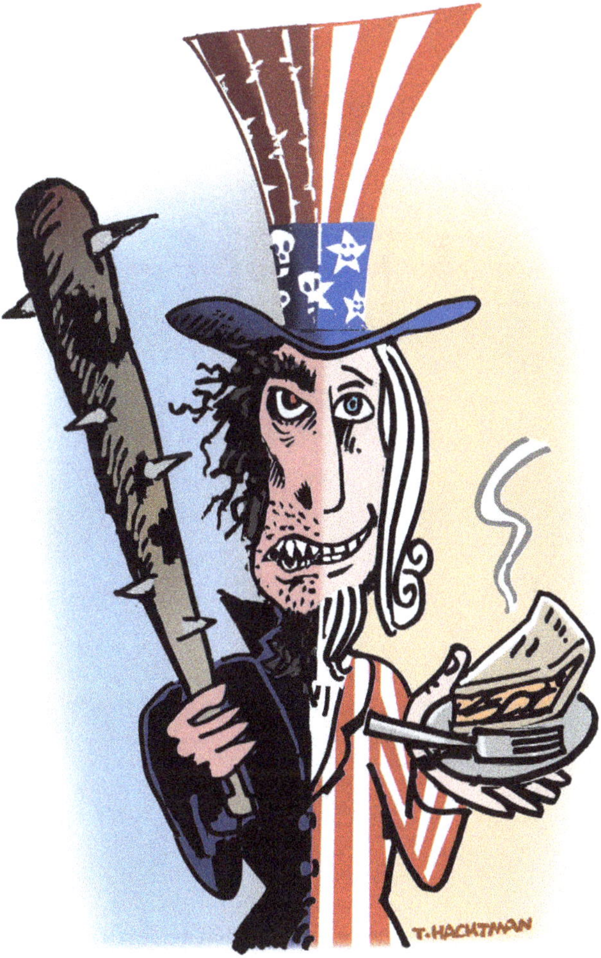
T. HACHTMAN

T. HACHTMAN

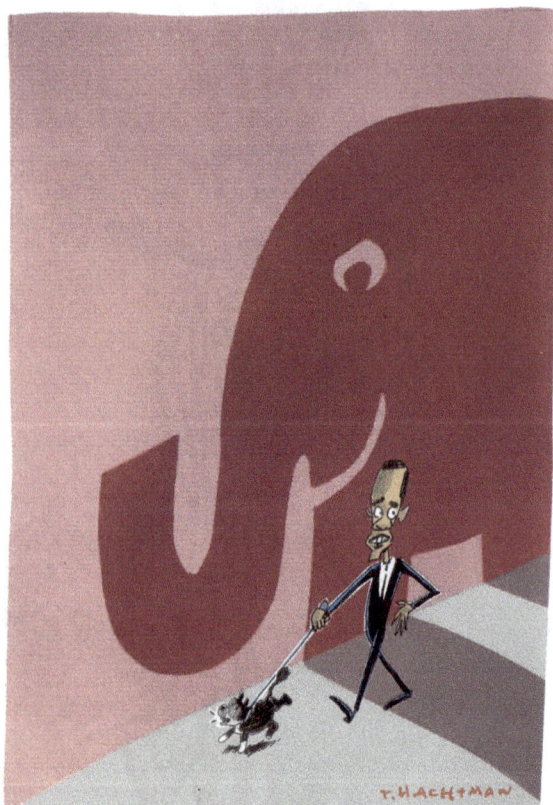

We don't expect you to be a great statesman

But don't be an obstructionist yob.

Enough with ridiculous rhetoric.

Just do your f**king job

Put ideological posing aside, dudes

Your refusal to legislate irks.

There are too many things that need doing,

To not get the f**k back to work.

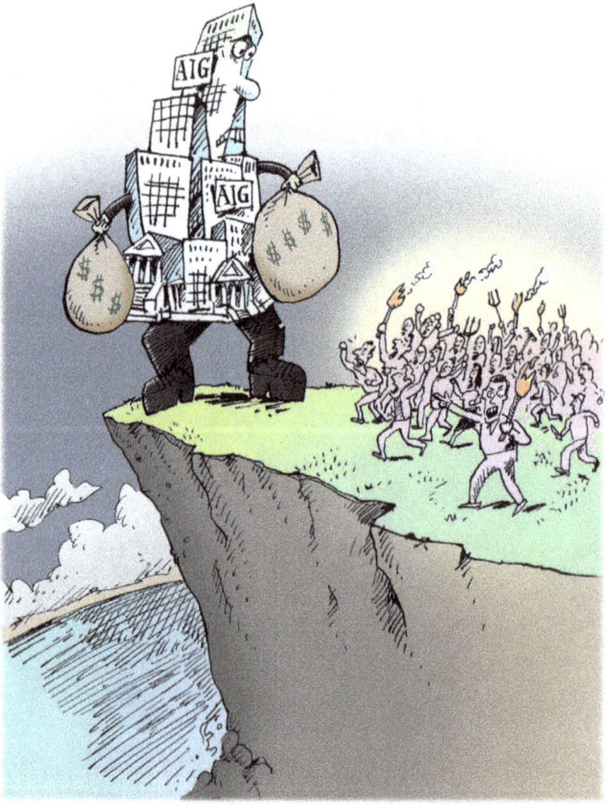
AIG
AIG

Having driven us nearly to ruin,

Constitutional duties you shirk.

We're just hanging on by our thumbs, here,

So, get the f**k back to work!

Popping one at a time from a clown car's

The right entrance for you half-witted twerps,

Even funny if when you got to your office,

You just did some f**king work.

Your election by roused home district rabble

Proves you're no inside-the-beltway snob.

Now show us you're not just a vandal

And go do your f**king job!

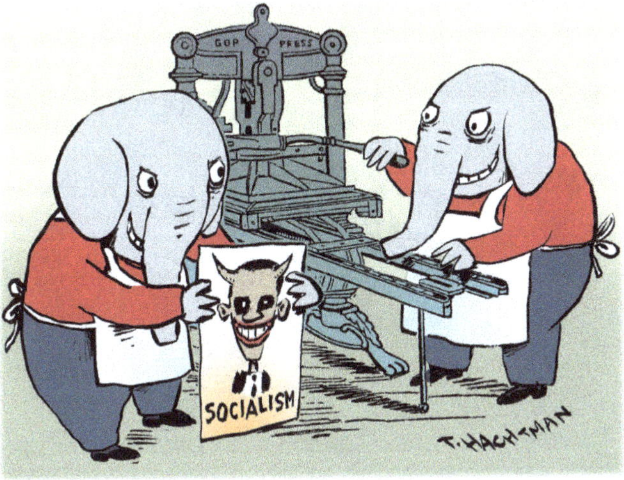
GOP PRESS
SOCIALISM
T. HACHTMAN

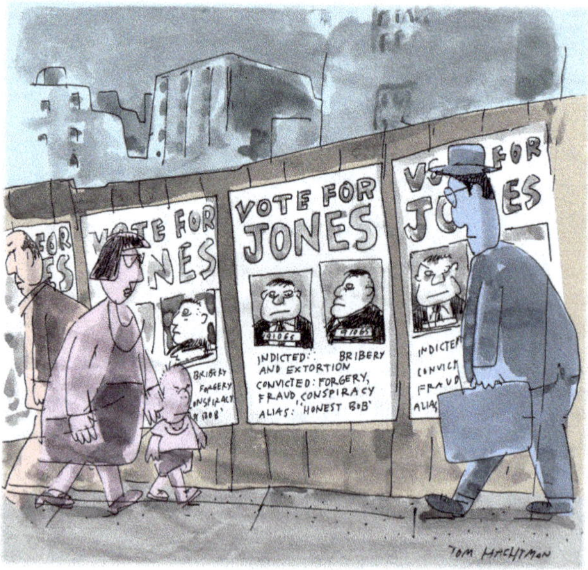
VOTE FOR JONES
INDICTED: BRIBERY AND EXTORTION
CONVICTED: FORGERY, FRAUD, CONSPIRACY
ALIAS: "HONEST BOB"
TOM HACHTMAN

It's heady, that rush of new power,

Especially for you younger turks,

But the country's in serious trouble,

So get the f**k back to work.

If a congressman came from Nantucket

Then turned into a party hack knob

His homeys would tell him to suck it

And just do his f**king job

If your plan all along was to do nothing,

You've succeeded, so wipe off those smirks.

Maybe now you could try something different,

Like going the f**k back to work!

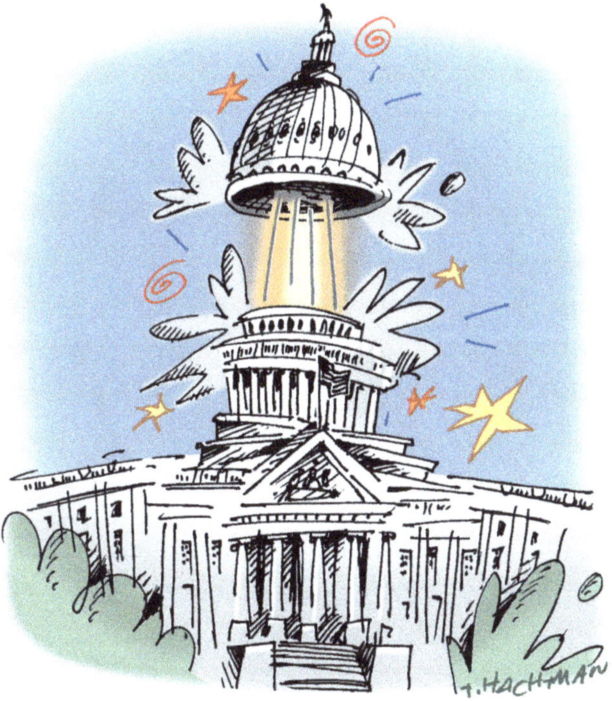
T. HACHMAN

www.ingramcontent.com/pod-product-compliance
Lightning Source LLC
Chambersburg PA
CBHW060747100426
42813CB00004B/726